HAPPY HOUR

First published in 2023 by 100 Movements Publishing
www.100Mpublishing.com
Copyright © 2023 by Hugh Halter

This book was originally published by Activus in 2016.

All Scripture quotations, unless otherwise indicated, are from the ESV®
Bible (The Holy Bible, English Standard Version®), copyright © 2001
by Crossway, a publishing ministry of Good News Publishers. Used by
permission. All rights reserved.

Scripture quotations marked NIV are taken from the Holy Bible, New
International Version®, NIV®. Copyright © 1973, 1978, 1984, 2011 by
Biblica, Inc.™ Used by permission of Zondervan. All rights reserved
worldwide. www.zondervan.com The "NIV" and "New International
Version" are trademarks registered in the United States Patent and
Trademark Office by Biblica, Inc.™

Scripture quotations marked KJV are taken from the King James Version.
Public domain.

ISBN: 978-1-955142-31-1 (print)
ISBN: 978-1-955142-32-8 (ebook)

Cover design by Revo Creative

100 Movements Publishing
An imprint of Movement Leaders Collective
Cody, Wyoming
www.movementleaderscollective.com
www.catalysechange.org

HAPPY HOUR

HUGH HALTER

ETIQUETTE
AND
ADVICE
ON HOLY
MERRIMENT

100 MOVEMENTS
PUBLISHING

MENU

HORS D'OEUVRE

AN INTRO INTO A LIFE OF CELEBRATION

Hi there, friends! Welcome to the next best season of your life! No, "an intro into a life of celebration" doesn't mean you can just "party" all the time, but as we'll talk about, God invites us into a rhythm of celebration, conversation, and community. Ever since creation, God has given his people a pattern for living. This pattern includes work, family, and sabbath, as well as festivals, feasts, and fellowships of every kind. Celebration is not just a part of life. It is the framework through which God's story is told to all people in every culture. Although some rhythms of life can create barriers for human interaction, celebration can transcend culture and connect disparate cultures together. To this day, the table, the home, the food, and the practice of hospitality remain the best way to bring people together and bring God into the room.

In the West, we live with annual rhythms such as Christmas, Thanksgiving, Easter, the Super Bowl, and other national times of celebration. But by and large we have forgotten the ancient art and the practice of weekly celebration and of deep hospitality. The party is God's way of helping us to remember him and keep him first, but it is also the way God can extend his blessing to the world.

For the Halters, "the party" was all we had. Or at least all we were left with. Although we felt called to a more traditional ministry lifestyle, our son, Ryan, and his hourly battle with grand mal seizures forced me out of seminary, and out of any normal life besides. Cheryl was locked down at home caring for him, as well as for our two daughters, and I had to go back to full-time work as a house painter just to survive. While we were buried in this daily struggle, we thought our divine "calling" to ministry had been revoked, or at least delayed. But it hadn't.

It all changed one fateful day, or at least that was when we started to figure out what God was doing. Over coffee, I was lamenting to Cheryl about our plight. Sleep deprived and tired of painting, I was upset that God seemed unaware of, or at least uninterested, in our struggle. I was frustrated that Cheryl didn't have much of a life, and I was sad that my heart to help people find faith in Jesus seemed a million miles away. Okay, I was pretty much just whining to Cheryl about how lame our life was.

In a moment of clarity, Cheryl said, "We can at least open our home, have people over for meals, and see what God does … can't we?"

Staring into my coffee, I thought, *Well, I suppose we could. And our brood has to eat at least twenty-one meals a week anyway, so … yeah, let's give it a go and maybe give a few meals away.*

With that small, divine conversation, our lives changed. Eventually, many other lives were changed as well. We started small by having just one party a week with a handful of friends, but the house quickly filled up. Without changing the mundane grind of working a normal job, managing family, or the obtrusive struggle of caring for a severely disabled son, we encouraged others to party well.

The result? A church was born in Portland.

Ten years later, we moved to Denver with all of the same struggles—no change at all, actually—and Cheryl reminded me again that we could open our home and party. We bought two rocking chairs from Walmart and had coffee on the front porch. Eventually that grew to "Happy Hours" with neighbors. Weekend parties continued, and, yep, the house filled up. And again, another church was born, this time with the intentional rhythms of party built into our discipleship process, as well as the natural flow of our lives. We figured that almost every friend who eventually found Jesus, first found themselves drawn into the festivities in a home.

Along with Matt Smay, I went on to write *The Tangible Kingdom,* which is all about the central way of living out the kingdom of God and making it tangible to others. At first, most of the people that read it were pastors struggling to keep their churches alive. We began consulting with churches across the country and around the world, and every time we assessed what was the biggest obstacle and the best opportunity for change, we had to admit that it came down to this: People weren't engaging the world with a good news life. Even more, most pastors had never been given permission or taught that a *missional life*—and therefore a *missional church*—hinges on being a *missionary saint*. And that central to this life is the Jesus-modeled element of the party.

So we wrote an eight-week guide for any normal Joe or Jolene. It's called the *TK Primer*, which, after eight weeks, leads the small group up to one big event …

Yep, you guessed it.

Throwing a party.

To our surprise, people by the thousands said, "Yes, that whole party thing was harder than I thought." Some shared how they didn't have non-believing friends, so they didn't know who to invite. Some shared the frustration that their spouse didn't like having people in the home. Some shared how awkward their small group Bible study was and how they would never trust their Christian friends with their unbelieving friends. Some spoke of their introversion, their exhaustion, and lack of energy for a party. And of course, many didn't think it was biblical to party, especially if alcohol was involved.

And so after ten years of being on the road trying to help churches, church leaders, and church people bring the gospel to the world, I now believe the one skill every believer must develop is the discipleship skill of throwing a great party. No, it's not just about outreach to lost friends. It's really about our discipleship after Jesus. If he did it, and we claim to follow him, then we must stretch past church attendance and Bible studies to learn how to be great human beings like he was.

So this is a book for *missionaries in a missionary context.*

Which is *all believers.*

(Yes, that means YOU!)

WHY THIS LITTLE BOOK?

First, because I don't think most of you have time to read the long book I wrote; and second, because I'd rather you get the basics and get moving instead of bottlenecked in reading. So *Happy Hour* is a simple book that will give you a little theology, a little missiology, a ton of stories, and all the best practices of how to throw a party Jesus would want to bring his friends to.

HOW TO USE THIS BOOK

This book is best used with your friends, small groups, or church-planting team. Trust me, you don't want to be the only one who can throw a great party. If your entire small group or tribe can catch the bug and create great parties, every ministry hope and dream you might have will be far easier. If you want to read *Happy Hour* within the context of a larger book on incarnational living, try reading one of my other books, *Flesh,* as a group and then add this little resource to the experience.

1

PARTY AS SACRAMENT

THE THEOLOGY AND MISSIOLOGY OF PARTY

The Son of Man has come eating and drinking,
and you say, "Look at him! A glutton and a
drunkard, a friend of tax collectors and sinners!"

LUKE 7:34

I don't know what your favorite Scripture is, but this is one of mine! You see, I've always been amazed at how counterintuitive Jesus was. That is, he almost always does the exact opposite of what religious people thought he should do. Back then and also today.

I'm not sure if you've noticed, but we have a lot of religion and a lot of Christians hanging around everywhere. Some people even think America is still a Christian nation because we have so many that would at least raise a hand to acknowledge some kind of belief. So with all of us "followers of Jesus," you would think the non-Christian world would love us.

But that is not the case.

Just for kicks, take a moment to Google "Christians are" and see what comes up. Not so good, right? Now Google "Jesus was." Totally different. Christians are perceived as rude, exclusive, homophobic, bigoted, racist, hypocritical, holier-than-thou. And those are the nicer comments!

So how come Jesus doesn't get tagged with all the negatives we do? Well, simply this: Jesus hung out with people that we don't, and he must have eaten a lot because the word on the street was that he was a drunk and a glutton, a friend of tax collectors and sinners. Yes, Jesus had some enemies (the religious people), but the peasants, prostitutes, plumbers, and publicans seemed to have been really drawn to him.

To put it simply, the least religious loved this non-religious rabbi.

Why did people call him a "friend of sinners?" Because he simply ate and drank with them.

The rest of the book will be about how you can follow suit, but first I think it will be helpful if we take a chapter to talk about the theology, missiology, and sociology of eating, since it is so central to the party.

THE THEOLOGY OF FOOD

Right now, you may be muttering, "Halter, come on. There's a theology of *food* and *party*?" Yes, indeed, there is! And it's connected with hospitality and friendship with sinners.

Let's first start with John 1:14. This one Scripture sets up the human life of Jesus as the primary example of how we are to live:

> *And the Word became flesh and dwelt among us, and we have seen his glory, glory as of the only Son from the Father, full of grace and truth.*

This is the story of Jesus in a nutshell, but it is also much more. It shows the *missiology* of Jesus—why and how he came to us. It shows the *sociology* of Jesus—how he postured himself, full of grace and truth, among us. It is the backdrop for all *evangelism*—it shows the power of being full of grace and truth. Thus it forms the *theological* idea of what God wants us to do—that we model the *incarnational* way of Jesus.

Being incarnational is your new permission slip to define holiness in a new way. Perhaps you've previously understood holiness as separating yourself or avoiding the world. Instead, if we let Jesus define holiness, it's about living a life set apart for God while also living a life that is deeply entrenched in the normal affairs of life. As Jesus prayed for his would-be world changers in John 17:15, "I do not ask that you take them out of the world, but that you keep them from the evil one."

In the ancient Middle Eastern context that Jesus was part of, to share a meal with someone automatically meant you accepted them. In fact, the Greek word for *hospitality* actually means "love of stranger." People were taught to allow travelers into their homes and care for them just like they would for a family member. Of course, some didn't. Just like today. And just like today, people didn't do what God commanded or Jesus showed. Instead, they developed some serious racial, social, political, economic, and religious reasons not to share a meal with someone. They only ate with those who agreed with them, worshipped at the same synagogue, ate the same foods, and knew well enough not to eat the wrong foods. They had strong theology, but they developed it through their own traditional interpretation of Scripture instead of through the lens of Jesus.

In Acts 10 we have the strongest example of this. Just for kicks, read the entire passage. I'll wait ...

Do you see how powerful eating a meal was? Peter, like most in his day, formed his religious elitism based on who he was or wasn't supposed to eat with and what was or wasn't supposed to be eaten. It was that simple. So for God to tell him to go against his upbringing, against long-held beliefs and traditional interpretations of Scripture, was not just going against the grain. To Peter, it actually felt like he was going against God.

Today, I have found we do the same thing. I grew up in a "holiness tradition" church. There are very beautiful aspects to a focus on holiness, the biggest of which is that when we give our lives to Jesus, he likes us to do a little cleaning up and try to align our lives more to his. But what often happens when we focus on external holiness is that we unconsciously move away from anything we think would be bad for us … especially certain types of people. For me, I couldn't go to the movie theater or skating rink because "bad things" happen there. I couldn't eat potato chips or drink too much pop because my body was the temple of the Holy Spirit—Jesus would never put bad food in his temple! As I got older, I was persuaded to throw my Led Zeppelin, Billy Idol, and U2 CDs away. (What a mistake that was!) You get the point.

Holiness for me was based on what I did or didn't do. But if we follow Jesus, and I mean really follow him, holiness actually *must* be based on how closely our lives are modeled after his. We may have been living as if holiness equates to not eating or drinking or having friends who are sinners. But if we follow Jesus, we must do those very things. His humanity must become our humanity, and we should have the same friends he would have had. If not, we may not be moving toward holiness.

THE SOCIOLOGY OF FOOD

Sociology is basically the study of how humans relate to other humans. Of course, humans have developed many hundreds, if not thousands, of unique cultures, so picking one way to relate to everyone isn't that plausible, *except* when it comes to food.

I'm not sure if we realize that the gospel of the kingdom of

God is a culture in and of itself. The reason Jesus was so excited about sharing the good news (gospel) was because it told the story that heaven was now possible here on earth, that the way things are in God's original created order can be visible here, now. This is why Jesus said, "Repent, for the kingdom of heaven is at hand" (Matthew 4:17). He was declaring that a new way of life was available to anyone who would stop living *their* way and instead live *his* way.

Heaven began to invade earth, and the culture of the gospel started to ooze into our human cultures. And since celebration, community, love, and food are so much a part of God's original design and heavenly reality, we have to learn to see food, family, homes, friends, and community through this new gospel lens. Jesus' gospel culture gets to win over every culture—including our own.

This is why Scripture says to "practice hospitality" (Romans 12:13 NIV). Practice implies we need to do a little work, blow the dust off, wade in up to our ankles, and at least give it a try.

Picture in your mind what good ole fashioned Midwestern values are. It's probably safe to say that most people picture good, wholesome, church-going folks who live life in the context of family. Sounds great, right? Well, as we were planting a church in Denver, we found these folks the toughest to move toward the mission of God. What got in the way? Sunday dinners with their family.

Alan and Debra Hirsch, missiologists and culture experts, rightly explain the problem in their book *Untamed:*

This is "our" space, and those we may "invite" into that space are carefully chosen based on whether they will upset the delicate status quo, inconvenience us, or pose a threat to our perceived safety. In other words, visitors, especially strange ones, stress us out. And while this is in some sense culturally understandable, the negative result in terms of our spirituality is that the family has effectively become a pernicious idol ... . Culture has once again trumped our social responsibility. In such a situation, missional hospitality is seen as a threat, not as an opportunity to extend the kingdom; so an idol is born. ... It's not hard to see how this is absolutely disastrous from a missional perspective. Our families and our homes should be places where people can experience a foretaste of heaven, where the church is rightly viewed as a community of the redeemed from all walks of life (Revelation 21). Instead, our fears restrict us from letting go of the control and safety we have spent years cultivating.

This is why I claim that party is sacrament. Sacraments are those deep, long-held practices that hold the church together and set her apart from the common fray. Like baptism, the

---

*   Alan Hirsch and Debra Hirsch, *Untamed: Reactivating a Missional Form of Discipleship* (Grand Rapids, MI: Baker Books, 2010), 166–167.

Lord's Supper, and marriage, I think Jesus would say, "Oh, and add one more thing I really want you all to do if you're going to be my disciples. I need you to throw the best parties on the block."

THE MISSIOLOGY OF FOOD

"And Jesus came eating and drinking" is not just a fun Scripture. It is both *why* and *how* Jesus came to earth. The why was to "seek and save the lost" (Luke 19:10). The how began with a meal.

Take a second to look again at that verse we began with in John 1:14. It shows what mission work is all about and what missionaries do if they take on the mission of Jesus.

For most folks, the incarnation is simply about Jesus coming to die for our sins. In this sense, he is our Savior. The story of what he did for us moves us to emotion and tears, and it compels us to be part of a church and to worship.

But he didn't just come to die for sins. He also came to teach us how to live and be human. He never intended to be just our Savior. He wants to be our Lord—the one who gets to run our lives. So we must let him come off the cross. This is why the word *disciple* is so important. A disciple is someone who studies and lives out what the Master believes and lived out. It's why the apostle Paul said, "I have been crucified with Christ. It is no longer I who live, but Christ who lives in me. And the life I now live in the flesh I live by faith in the Son of God, who loved me and gave himself for me" (Galatians 2:20).

Paul was saying, "I don't get to call the shots anymore or live simply in the comfort zone of what I like." Paul was to become the great missionary apostle, traveling from town to town, propelled by worship, but also compelled to follow Jesus into the missionary context he was called to.

And like Paul, we have received the same theology, the same sociology, and the same missiology. Jesus said it this way, "As the Father has sent me, even so I am sending you" (John 20:21). And so, if Jesus came eating and drinking, and some called him a drunk and a glutton and a friend of sinners, then we should do the same things and get the same reputation he did.

In Jesus, you have an example, a mandate, an opportunity, a calling, and a permission slip to stop being religious, to go enjoy life, and to live like a missionary.

Cheers!

2

PUBLIC HOUSE

HOW TO PARTY AT HOME

Cheryl and I have fixed up about twelve homes in our thirty years of life together. Most of the time we did it because we relied on the income from the ole fix-'n-flip to survive the vicissitudes of life. But the other reason was a simple love of creating places of belonging for others. If you've ever read one of my earlier books, *The Tangible Kingdom*, the entire story takes place in a home we bought in a suburb of Denver. Cheryl and I had moved from Portland to Denver, and after looking for a whole week, we realized the market was just too expensive. One night, Cheryl gave up sadly and went to bed, but I couldn't let it go. I stayed up late, looking through websites for defunct real estate and found a home that was almost condemned just a mile away from where we were staying. It looked promising! As Cheryl slept, I snuck out to the car and drove to check the joint out, flashlight in hand. It was beautiful from the outside, but the inside was trashed. Really trashed.

The next morning at 5:30 a.m., before Cheryl woke up, I drove to see it again in the daylight. The contractor was there putting stilts on the front so they could pour a new foundation. I walked up and said, "Hey, would you take $205k for it as is ... I mean, 'as is' once you pour a new foundation?" He stood up, took a few puffs on his Swisher Sweet cigar, and said, "Yep."

We shook hands, and I went back, woke Cheryl up, and said, "Honey, I just bought a house." Disoriented but a little excited (that's what I love about her), I took her up the hill to see it. As we drove, she commented on how nice the neighborhood was, but I could see she was still skeptical. As we pulled up, I started to get out to show her, but she didn't get out of the car. As I bent down to talk to her through the car window, all she asked was, "Can you fix it?" I said, "Of course, Babe. I got this." And with that, the deal was made. We flew back to Portland, and then a couple of weeks later I flew out by myself to begin the thirty-five-day renovation before the family joined me.

Like the prophet Nehemiah staring at the rubble of Jerusalem after its demolition, so I found myself walking through the home, trying to get a vision for what would fit our family and the new mission we were embarking on; the mission of seeing new friends find faith in Jesus.

So where did I start? The very first thing I did was tear out the big dividing wall separating the living room from the family room and another wall from the family room to the kitchen. I opened everything up. It cost me a lot to reroute electrical and hang a $2000 steel I-beam that would span the entire length of the home, but I knew if it worked, it would open the house up, making it possible to seat fifty people. Well, it worked, and that one big room was the single most important factor in our ability to throw a great party.

So as we get started, let's talk about how to have an "Open Home."

GO AND PREPARE

In John 14:1–3, Jesus tells his disciples he is leaving them. No doubt, they are feeling sad and disappointed. He tries to encourage them by saying that even though he's going away, he's going to prepare a place for them so they can always be with him: "In my Father's house are many mansions: if it were not so, I would have told you. I go to prepare a place for you" (John 14:2 KJV). Maybe they didn't feel that encouraged at the time, but if they had understood what he was really talking about, I think they would have been.

Jesus was talking about literally preparing a home where they could all live together. Unlike our suburban architecture, which is often constructed so that people can be separate and unseen, Jesus' vision was classically Middle Eastern. In those days and in that culture, a father would simply add on to an existing home to make room for his kids as they went off, married, and then returned. Mansions weren't ornate behemoths behind gated fences as we might picture. Instead, the idea of the *mansion* was a home that was continually enlarged to make room for "the family" to live life together.

So consider some re-architecting. No, you don't have to tear down walls and put in I-beams, but you can if you want. Consider your home, and ask yourself these questions:

- How many people can we fit comfortably?
- Are there any flow issues that could be changed? That is, when people are in our home, can they flow easily from the front door to the kitchen, dining room, living room, back porch?
- If not, what could we do to "open it up?"
- Are there any rooms we're not presently using? If so, how could they be incorporated into hospitality?
- How could we specifically make the kitchen the easiest room to see and to get to? (Most people no longer enjoy a formal dining room. Instead they like an open design where the kitchen opens up to more casual dining opportunities.)
- How could we reconsider the colors in our home? (Color helps set the mood, so take some time to check out the latest home magazines for ideas. The writers and contributors often talk about the psychology of color and arrangement, so you may get some great ideas.)

MAKE READY

In John 1:19–28, John the Baptist tells the priest and Levites that his job was to "make straight the way of the Lord"(v.23). He was to get people ready to meet Jesus. That means we too should consider all the ways we can make it easier for people to be receptive to meet Jesus. How can we help them enter, connect, enjoy, share their story, and pick up on our story? All these things are part of the "art of making ready." Check out these great ways to perfect this art:

Pre-Party

The pre-party prep is as important as the party itself. You are setting the atmosphere, which sets the stage for either a warm, wonderful gathering or a train wreck. Trust me, you'll prefer the former!

- *Do* clean the house. People can feel uncomfortable coming into an environment that says, "Oh, I wasn't expecting you." A clean home shows people you knew they were coming, and you prepared a place for them.
- *Don't* have the TV on (unless they are coming over to watch a game). When the TV is on, people will gravitate toward it because they can stare at a screen and not relate to folks around them. It will also be the place your most socially awkward people go, so why oh why would you want a herd of those people all sitting down together? The TV also compels people to find a

seat too fast. Parties are best when people are standing and getting to know each other.

- **Do** have soft music on. Like food, music is always a winner … unless you put on bad music! What I'm trying to say is, "Don't put on Christian music!" (Just kidding … sort of.) If you play Christian music, some will think you are doing the classic bait-and-switch thing and are subtly trying to put them in a Jesus trance. Try to play music that's appropriate to the audience. Stick with music like light jazz, folk and singer-songwriter, or coffee shop rock. Even "oldy" riffs like Sinatra can really spiff up the mood. Go for anything that creates nice background conversation tones. In other words, nothing so heavy that it becomes a distraction. Keep the volume to where it is noticeable but not hard to talk over. This is your home, not a nightclub.
- **Do** have scented candles lit, especially in the bathroom and main sitting room. They create a cozy atmosphere. Aroma is also important in setting a warm atmosphere.

What About the Kids?

This is the question I hear most. Probably because if you've had kids, you'll know they are the element most likely to screw up a great evening. (Kidding, but not really.) They can poop their pants, throw a hissy fit, punch another kid in the face, or simply get uncomfortable and start crying for no other reason than to challenge your faith in Jesus! So *always*, and I mean *always*, find ways ahead of time to relieve their stress and prepare them for the night to come.

- ***Do*** talk with children ahead of time to let them know how you'd like them to help out with the party. Ask them to get their toys ready to share, and help them make the other kids feel comfortable by taking them downstairs to watch a nice show, play video games, or whatever. If you're going to have any adult conversation time, let them know that after dinner you're going to ask them to hang out with the other kids.
- ***Caveat:*** If you have toddlers, all bets are off. I'd still suggest you do what you can to make straight the way of the Lord, but when they freak, just prepare your heart so you don't throw them through the wall. That's what we call a party foul.

Honestly, the best thing you can do is to make sure you've got the house clean at least an hour in advance so you and your spouse can have time with the kids, get them as ready as you can, pray, and prepare your soul for whatever happens. Remember that one of the unique witnesses of the gospel is how a family functions under stress, so keep a sense of humor, and try to communicate through as many of the things that can go wrong as possible.

Party Time

Okay, it's now time to party. Consider these pointers as people come in:

Threshold. This means the "place or point of beginning" and is the first moment you have to set your guests at ease and is the spot where people feel least comfortable. Standing and staring at a front door feels like when you get to a packed DMV office when the air conditioning has failed. It's just weird. And here's what most people think while waiting: *I hope we didn't come too early! I hope we didn't come too late! I wonder if this is the right night? I wonder if they got in a big fight today and wish they had cancelled? I wonder if I have a booger sticking out! I hope their kids aren't freaking out.*

Turn the lights on. Seriously, a well-lit front porch is very inviting, whereas a poorly lit or barely lit front stoop says, "Vampires live here. Abandon hope all ye who enter."

Keep the door cracked. Since waiting outside a closed door is uncomfortable, I always like to at least crack it or, in warmer weather, open it completely. And if I'm not tied up preparing food, I've found it much easier to be right there waiting for everyone and actually come out onto the front porch to meet folks. It breaks the ice and makes people think you're so excited to have them over that you've been waiting. If you're doing this in community (as you should), invite two to three people to come early just to be helpers and greeters. If a non-homeowner answers and introduces themselves, it helps the rookies realize they are not the only guests, making their comfort levels go through the roof. (PS: The people answering the door should be your most relational people, not the awkward TV watchers.)

Invite them in. Communicate how glad you are that they are in your home. Right away, ask them if you can take their coat or personal items. Let them know exactly where they will be kept.

Have some finger food, coffee, tea, assortments of drinks already out. In any Middle Eastern context, food is thrust into your hands and face as soon as you come in. New folk are often the first ones there because they don't want to experience the pain of walking into a full home. The invitation to eat and drink helps relieve their initial awkwardness. I find that if I ask, "Would you like something to drink or snack on?" they often say no out of politeness. So instead have a drink or small plate in your hand and say, "What can I get you? Oh, you've got to try these, as well." If you make the choice for them to eat and drink, they will not have to try to figure out what's appropriate or not.

Introduce them to other guests. As soon as possible, I suggest you try to introduce them to as many other folks as you can. I often ask what they'd like to drink, and then on my way to get it, I'll make a few introductions, and make sure they are off and running on the conversation before I go get their drink. Then I'll return and join the conversation.

Informalities of Formalities

In most parties, everything leads up to the mealtime. Often as you move from informal hors d'oeuvres to the meal, people start to tighten up. Here are a few thoughts to make it easier:

- **Don't** pray before the meal. Again, people will feel like you are trying to trick them.

- **Do,** however, invite people together around the kitchen or wherever you are serving and give a warm welcome. Say something like, "Hey, friends, gather around. Before we eat, Cheryl and I just want to let you know we're really glad you're in our home. Some of you we've known for a long time, and some of you we've just been blessed to have met recently. Regardless, we feel honored you have come over."

- **Do** give an introduction to the food: "Just so you know, the main entrees are brook trout almondine and some meatloaf. But the other food—the gluten-free, dairy-free, vegan stuff—is over there." And then explain what the other food is. The more detail you give, the less stress people will feel if they do have food issues (which many people do nowadays). The last thing you want is a six-year-old swelling up like a blowfish because you forgot to mention the peanuts you snuck in the cookies. The more fun you can have with the introduction to the food, the better the experience will be.

- ***Do*** give a blessing or toast. Out of courtesy you won't pray, but out of love you can at least give a toast or blessing. Both are culturally relevant, create a warm feeling, and often provide a deep sense of togetherness. Sometimes, right after introducing the food, I'll say, "So let's raise our glasses tonight and toast to gratefulness over all the blessings we presently have in our lives, for the gift of food and friendship, a warm home and peace tonight." In saying that, you'll notice I am able to communicate a lot of deep thoughts without overwhelming people with a religious experience they may not be used to. Other times, I may actually prepare a short reading of a blessing or an Irish toast that is both fun and meaningful.

3

PARTY FAVORS

IT'S FIVE O'CLOCK SOMEWHERE

've heard it a hundred times: "You guys throw the best parties." To me, that's as great a compliment as when someone says, "I really loved the sermon today." Every party is different, and I've learned that the best parties are the ones with the right people at the right time. So, in this chapter I want to do you a favor and talk through the different party options you have. As I've traveled the world, I've come across unique party ideas, so find a few that best fit you and the people you want to serve.

HAPPY HOUR

The great theologian duo of Jimmy Buffett and Alan Jackson taught us a universal truth: It's five o'clock somewhere. Everywhere, all over the world, people have learned that unwinding after a long day is a really nice way to get their minds off the daily grind—something simple, relaxing, and fun. Sitting down for a long, formal, five-course meal is certainly not what they are looking for. It requires too much time and prep and making arrangements for the kids, not to mention the money! A fast, no-prep option is just the ticket. Enter Happy Hour!

Cheryl and I learned to bring Happy Hour into our house simply because Ryan's constant seizures wouldn't allow us to go out. When we bought those two rocking chairs from Walmart, we also brought the grill from the backyard and put it on the front porch with the chairs. Then, like good missionaries, we went out front, somewhere between four and five in the afternoon—the time most of our neighbors were coming home from work. As people saw us sipping a drink or standing over a smoking cooktop, it was quite natural for us to wave and say, "Steve … if you've got a few moments, come on over for a quick snack."

To make Happy Hours work, all you need is some simple finger foods, like cheese and crackers, and some simple drink options. A nice coffee drink is good in the winter, and summertime lends itself well to iced tea or lemonade, as well as a cold beer or sangria.

LIMING

Liming is a Caribbean term for party. The word is associated with sitting under a lime tree or having nothing more to do than squeezing limes. Because it is an experience that originated in warmer climates, it gives us some ideas for outside parties. I like this because, whether you live in a hot climate or a place like Denver, folks seem more at ease "outside" the home. Perhaps that's because people sometimes feel like an imposition inside someone else's house. In the Caribbean, all you need is a cheap fold-out chair. In Colorado, a nice gas fireplace is a good option. No matter where I have lived (or will), I've always built a firepit. People are always drawn to them, they can come and go without the same formalities as coming to and leaving a home, and men seem far more open to talk when they can stare at the flames instead of staring into each other's eyes. Seriously, give it a try.

POTLUCK

Most of you know what this is. It's simply a gathering where everyone brings a dish to share. I love this option because it is far less expensive, people love participating, you have more options, and you learn a lot about people by what they bring.

Some great ideas to spruce up a potluck are to organize it around a theme. You could declare "South of the Border Night!" or "Slow Cook Saturday!" or even "Vegan Friday!" depending on the people you're connecting with.

DINNER CLUB

The dinner club is, of course, dinner, but it works only when you call people to do it together. A basic starter is to ask three to six couples to commit to a year-long dinner club.

Once a month you get babysitters for the kids (maybe pitch in all together) and take turns going to one of the couple's homes. (Did I say without the kids?) The couple that hosts is responsible to cook the meal. And I don't mean take-out! This forces a natural competitive experience that is sure to be the best night of your month. It's like a date night with friends without the cost or hassle of going out. Your biggest prep is to unload the kids and spend a night together cooking and eating.

The meal must include five elements to be considered epic!

- **Hors d'Oeuvres:** This is a mid-eighteenth-century French term that literally means "outside the work." Not sure why, because hors d'oeuvres require some work (even if it's opening a jumbo package of Lil Smokies from Costco), but whatever—they're always an important warm-up for the main event.
- **Drink Pairings:** In most cultures, the drink is as important as the food. If you're from the South, try to break free of sweet tea; if you're from the Northwest, not everyone likes microbrews. Try to learn and offer unique beverages that pair well with what you're serving. If you're not sure, Google it.
- **Main Course:** That's the big show!
- **Dessert:** Does this really need a description?
- **Night Cap:** Usually a coffee drink or a port, cognac, or whiskey.

BRAAI

If you want to dip your toe into a deeper food experience, I love to highlight the South African tradition of a *braai*, which is an extended food experience with the entire family that often covers a time span of two meals. When I was in Pretoria in the early '90s, I was invited to a home with five other families. The *braai* began at ten in the morning with a brunch-type of fair. But then the barbeques lit up, and for the next six hours, we just sat around, talked, cooked, nibbled, talked some more, played some games, cooked some more, and on and on. This is a great way to deepen relationships and get really fat but is well worth it.

HOW TO GO TO A PARTY

So far we've talked mostly about how to throw a party in your own home. But there's another side to that coin: What are some things you should do when you are invited *to* a party?

First, come and leave at an appropriate time. I was throwing a St. Patty's Day party once, and a dude from another state saw my Facebook post to our church community and actually bought a plane ticket and showed up. That was weird enough, but more annoying was that he showed up an hour early. *Never, never, never* show up early! Most hosts will be scurrying around at the last minute trying to get everything ready, and the last thing they need to is to try to entertain early guests while doing a last-minute vacuum or yelling at the kids to help.

Likewise, never stay too late. Whenever we've thrown a party, I've often ended the evening wanting to bash someone over the head because they've decided to be the last one out. In most cases, parties have what I call the "final bow," where four, five, or six of the last people all bow out together, saying something like, "Okay, well it looks like the party's just about over, so thanks for having us!" When you hear or see this final group leave, that's your cue to join 'em! It's a respectful gesture to your hosts who have spent a good part of the day getting their home ready and then spent the evening entertaining the gathering. By the end of the evening, they're probably pretty tuckered out, so don't overstay your welcome.

What's the best time to come and go? As a general rule, unless they specify a starting time or a dinner time as "sharp," I like to come about fifteen to twenty minutes after the beginning bell and then leave as most people leave at the end. The only reason I may stay a little later is to help clean up, wash dishes, or help the hosts close up shop.

Second, always bring a gift. I almost always bring a bottle of wine, other drinks, a candle, or flowers. It doesn't take much to stop and pick something up, but you will stand out from the crowd, and it will be a huge blessing to the hosts.

Third, try to be a greeter for them and take some pressure off the hosts who have to do everything else. As other people come in, consider being the door guy or gal, invite guests in, introduce yourself, find out how they are connected with the hosts, and lend your warmth into their home.

4

PARTY KILLERS

HOW NOT TO CROSS THE LINE

So, can I be honest? I love Irish whiskey. I even have an Irish pub in my home. But you know what else? I don't drink it very often, and out of all the parties I've thrown, I very rarely offer it to others.

As I've spoken and taught people around the world to party, one of the most asked questions is, "What about the booze? Should Christians drink it, offer it, avoid it, condemn it, or develop a taste for it?"

Well, let's start with Jesus. Here's what we know for sure: He drank it. In those days, there weren't the myriad options we have today. There was water, but it could kill you, so they had wine. Fermented drink, wine, early renditions of beer, and anything else they could ferment were safest and the most widely consumed beverage options. Wine held additional religious and social benefits. It was considered a blessing, and it was deeply symbolic of God's provision, presence, and blessing. As the gospel spread, people had to learn that many of the food and beverages they did or did not consume were not important to the new gospel of grace. As I mentioned earlier, Christians have often focused on being set apart or holier than the average person. But this pursuit of holiness often hindered people from enjoying things God gave us to enjoy. So Paul wrote,

> *For the kingdom of God is not a matter of eating and drinking, but of righteousness, peace and joy in the Holy Spirit, because anyone who serves Christ in this way is pleasing to God and receives human approval. Let us therefore make every effort to do what leads to peace and to mutual edification.*
>
> Romans 14:17–19 NIV

Another way to explain this is to say that God didn't want them to focus on simply being "set apart" but also on being "sent." What God did with Peter and Cornelius, and what Paul is saying here, helps us navigate between the two extremes. In Jesus' mind and Paul's, we are to be set apart—"not getting drunk with wine" but also not letting food or drink limit our ability to be sent as missionaries.

Jesus taught that there is nothing wrong with beer or wine, but he also taught us a few things to make sure our choices don't tilt us toward the dark side:

First, as a general rule, if you can keep it from being an issue during a party, you win. Alcohol will be an issue by saying either, "We don't have any alcohol in our home," or "We love alcohol." Both are rooted in a judgment you've made and thus can kill a party.

Think like a missionary. If you are a missionary in Spain, Italy, Australia, or France, to not have a drink is a terrible missionary posture. It is just part of the culture. Likewise, if you are called to the UK, you'd better learn to like some tea and port. If you're called to Portland or Denver, you'd be wise to develop a taste for microbrews, specifically IPAs. Alcohol is part of our new American missionary culture, and although you don't have to drink, Jesus gives you permission to.

THE BIG CAVEAT

The one big caveat about booze is that it can and does destroy lives, and many people really struggle with it.

After saying that everything is acceptable, Paul continues:

Do not destroy the work of God for the sake of food. All food is clean, but it is wrong for a person to eat anything that causes someone else to stumble. It is better not to eat meat or drink wine or to do anything else that will cause your brother or sister to fall.

Romans 14:20–21 NIV

This really helps us find a good balance. Here are some practical examples of Paul's teaching in action:

- Don't force people beyond their consciences, and that includes everyone, from Christians who don't want any booze because their eighteen-year-old was killed by a drunk driver to those who are recovering alcoholics.
- Don't pressure people to eat or drink anything that may hurt them. That includes a cream puff for a diabetic or two fingers of scotch for an alcoholic.
- If the first two points above aren't an issue, then don't make one. Learn to enjoy.
- Enjoy in moderation. Where's the line? It's where you can enjoy a drink without social behavior becoming awkward or losing feeling in your face!

MORE CONSIDERATIONS

What if someone is an alcoholic? If they are, and many will be, they won't usually expect you to avoid alcohol. Every time an alcoholic goes out to eat, they are in an environment where alcohol is available. Part of their healing process is learning to navigate life, food, and community without saying yes to a drink. So offering it in your home does not usually cause them to sin or harm them. I have many friends who are recovering alcoholics, and most have told me that they would feel weird if I did not offer booze to my guests just because they were going to be there.

What if someone goes overboard or has one too many? I'll be honest and say that after throwing hundreds of parties, I can count on one hand the times I've noticed a friend over the limit. In almost every case, I've simply gone to them, handed them a glass of water, and said, "Chill out. I don't want you to be sick tomorrow." In most of these cases, they got the point, and some even thanked me for calling an end to their drinking. On the one occasion someone got out of control, I invited them outside and let them know I was going to have a friend drive them home. I don't ever feel it is useful to confront someone who is "lit," but I did go to his home the next day to see how he was feeling, and the conversation turned to some life issues he really needed a hand with. When I offered to help, he felt blessed not only that I took care of him, but also that I was willing to walk through his struggle with him.

I wasn't glad he had one too many, but, as this story illustrates, responding appropriately can be a great point of ministry to someone.

So why do so few people go over the line? Because they see me, my family, and my friends all enjoy a glass or a pint without going overboard. Positive peer pressure is more powerful than negative peer pressure, and over the years, so many people have commented on how we are the most fun people they know even though we've never gone overboard. *That* is the gospel, my friends. "The kingdom is not a matter of eating and drinking" means that the kingdom of God is seen as people notice the subtle but visible nuances of how we party well.

5

THE LAST CALL

THE BEST PARTY I'VE EVER THROWN

I t was late into a St. Patty's Day party when a couple I'd never met until that night asked, "So do you guys believe in that Easter thing?" They had been invited by some other friends of ours to attend a classic bash we were throwing for about seventy-five people. The night was easy to host. People were already going to party somewhere, but for some reason they showed up at our place. The invitation read:

> *To all friends both old and never met yet, please join us at our casa for a night to revel in green beer, good friends, great music, and a five-minute message on "The Real St. Patrick." Come anytime from 6–7pm, but if you're late you'll miss a special St. P's Blessing.*

A lot of people came, and I was surprised to see so many new faces. A bunch of buddies and I had prepared some classic Irish fare, we had all the green beer tastefully displayed, and there were green lights and Irish décor throughout our home and outdoor patios. A fire was burning inside as well as outside in our firepit. A playlist of Irish music filled the air with jovial riffs, and of course I was wearing my classic Guinness man-apron. After several hours, the place was maxed out, so I blew a whistle and invited everyone to cram into our living room. Every square inch was taken up by humans God was allowing us to get to know. As I told everyone that we would begin the St. Patty's Day talk in two minutes, I had some friends pass out some Irish blessings, some Scripture, and some funny off-color Irish sayings. I then taught people the concept of a "blessing" and tied that into a brief, albeit brilliant, historical picture of the "man that saved Ireland."

At the close of the message, I told them I had given them all some type of blessing and asked everyone to quiet down as people read them one by one. When something funny was read, you could feel the levity dispel any remaining tension in the room. When something meaningful was read, you could see people think and ponder deeper thoughts. And when a scriptural blessing was read, I saw couples hold hands and even tears flow down cheeks.

As I looked into the faces of the friends who had helped me host the party, and who knew the real reason we did this, they smiled at me, my wife winked, and we—the host community—enjoyed the incredible privilege of once again seeing God show up at a party big time.

As people left, the new couple I mentioned before turned around and asked their question about Easter.

"Yeah, we do," I said, giving them a curious look.

"Well, you guys should throw another party next week on Easter and invite us all back."

So with that, we did. Except there were too many people, and we had to rent out an events center. We sent an email to this same seventy-five people and told them we would have a simple family gathering to share the Easter story and share a meal together. Around 125 people showed up, all because we threw a great party first.

I kicked off that party with a quote from my buddy Alan Hirsch. He says that "party is sacrament." What he means, and what I've seen countless hundreds of times, is that out of all the things we think are marks of the church—sacred elements or traditions we should hold dear, like baptism, communion, Christmas or Easter celebrations—a simple party is a place where heaven and earth come together. The party isn't an end in itself, but it is a huge beginning that sometimes ends with someone putting their faith in Jesus.

THE GOAL OF A PARTY

So with all the focus on party, what actually is the goal? For me, it's simple: People will want to party again. I've come to realize that the spiritual growth of any person is a long process.

The conversion of the heart and soul never happens overnight. People often find God because they first found God's people. Belonging therefore leads to believing, so the party is the pathway for social and spiritual connection.

Party develops and sustains the life of the community, and if people find friends, great conversation, a safe place to be themselves and to bring other friends to, then you have the makings of kingdom movement. If someone finds you through the party, then finding God will be much easier for them because they will already have a community of people to walk with.

So let your goal be to create a place where people always experience warmth, balance in food and drink, great conversation, and leave certain that they were known, seen, and invited to return.

IS IT THAT EASY?

"Okay, Hugh, so you just throw great parties and then people come to Jesus?" *No*, not even close. But the party is almost always the first chapter in that story. The later chapters are like a fine, white tablecloth meal with six courses. From the party, we move to conversation, and in conversation we find out what people's lives are like, what they like to do, and we get an idea of how we can connect again. Many we party with eventually become true friends with whom we share life, with its many experiences, pains, and pleasures. Then, in the context of sharing life in community, these new friends begin to notice our unique life brought about by our faith. They watch us live differently, and then they naturally converse with us about our lives and our faith. They ask questions, and we sit out on the porch and speak of Jesus without any weird pressure or time constraints. The party was our first time together, but we have the rest of our lives to see what God does. And just like Jesus with Levi and all the tax collectors, or Jesus reclining with the religious leaders, or Peter in Cornelius's home, or Paul in Priscilla and Aquila's home, something always seems to happen when a home is open, a table is set, and people honor and accept each other through hospitality and presence.

WHEN PARTY GETS PERSONAL

I know I've shared a lot about my family, but let me leave you with something even more personal—that is the tax and toll, as well as the benefits, of living a life of celebration. You see, I've always been an introvert. That means *I've had to decide to host* hundreds of parties—and I have to struggle mightily with myself. Every. Single. Time. As you recall, most of the time we were tired, overworked, and under resourced to live this life due to Ryan's epilepsy. But we did manage to encourage each other toward this "extra credit" way of living. Sometimes Cheryl was tired, and I would lift her up and say, "Don't worry, Babe. I'll get the house clean." Other times she would be the one encouraging me. We hardly ever wanted to throw the party, but we found that when it was over, we were always glad we did.

The greatest benefit was seeing the power of God. When you watch strangers become friends, friends become close friends, and then some of those friends find faith in Jesus, it's simply the best thing in the world! So, for this reason alone, I can encourage you to go the extra mile, even when you don't feel like it, because it will be a crucial part of your own spiritual formation. You will grow as you see God show up!

If you're introverted like me, take heart. Introversion and extroversion are not categories that determine whether or not we will be good or bad at partying. They're more about how a person recovers from energy given to people. And I can tell you from experience that you can only survive as a Party Animal if you see and construct your life around community. Cheryl and I may have got the parties going, but very quickly we had a community of friends who were always on our side and often took the weight of the gathering for us. As you party in community, you'll start to feel that parties are not events but simply a rhythm of life, and when you get to that point, I think you'll hit a stride you've always hoped to achieve.

I always remind myself, that I have been crucified with Christ, so it is no longer Hugh who gets to live his own life, but Christ who gets to gently pull Hugh beyond his comfort zone, perceived energy levels, and selfish whims.

So go. Let Jesus live your life, and you'll find your home will be more open, your small groups more celebrative. With a critical mass of us, our churches will be full of great, fun people rather than of lemon-faced curmudgeons, and we'll get to see the kingdom of God in our kitchens and around our firepits.

As I end this small resource on the etiquette of pious imbibing, I want to leave you with one last partying shot and a final toast.

The word "libation" actually refers to pouring out the first sip of one's drink to the gods with an invocation. But don't let that freak you out. Christians were also known to clink their glasses together after the first pour, and the noise made from the glasses connecting was supposed to mimic the sound of church bells and drive away demons.

So I raise my glass to you and pray that God will open your heart so that you will open your home. I pray that your rooms will be filled with friends, laughter, warmth, and cheer, and that the food you serve will fill hearts and change souls.

FURTHER RESOURCES

For more about living an incarnational life, I encourage you to check out some of my other books:

Flesh: Bringing the Incarnation Down to Earth
Righteous Brood: Making the Mission of God a Family Story
Sacrilege: Finding Life in the Unorthodox Ways of Jesus
The Tangible Kingdom: Creating Incarnational Community

Discover more at:
hughhalter.com
lifeasmission.co

ABOUT THE AUTHOR

Hugh Halter and his wife, Cheryl, have been missionaries in North America for more than thirty years. They've planted two churches and in 2016 founded Lantern Network in Alton, Illinois. Lantern Network is a kingdom ecosystem committed to incubating good works and benevolent businesses to bless the city. Hugh speaks extensively across the globe, encouraging innovative forms of church, and when home loves to help Cheryl run Rí Beag Refuge, an eighty-acre equine therapy farm. Hugh is a leading missional voice, authoring such books as *The Tangible Kingdom: Creating Incarnational Community*, *AND: The Gathered and Scattered Church*, and *Flesh: Bringing the Incarnation Down to Earth*. Hugh's most recent book is *Righteous Brood: Making the Mission of God a Family Story*, part of the Life as Mission Series, which seeks to equip Christians to live the missionary life of Jesus in their everyday context. Look out for future offerings from the Life as Mission Series!

Life as Mission Series

Resources that equip Christians to live the missionary life of Jesus in their everyday context.

Look out for other offerings in the Life as Mission Series.
Go to **lifeasmission.co**

Words Create Worlds

Want to buy bulk copies of *Happy Hour*?

By purchasing bulk copies from us, you are not only getting a better price per book, but you are also helping us to:

- ✅ Invest in training and equipping the church through insightful resources
- ✅ Support and publish authors from the global church
- ✅ Give voice and platform to emerging authors

Unlock Imagination. Release Potential.